I0787041

WAITT, WHAT?

REFLECTIONS ON GLOBAL POLITICS

SAMUEL WAITT

WestBow Press books may be ordered through booksellers or by contacting:

WestBow Press
A Division of Thomas Nelson & Zondervan
1663 Liberty Drive
Bloomington, IN 47403
www.westbowpress.com
844-714-3454

ISBN: 979-8-3850-3830-5 (sc)
ISBN: 979-8-3850-3831-2 (hc)
ISBN: 979-8-3850-3829-9 (e)

Library of Congress Control Number: 2024924462

Print information available on the last page.

WestBow Press rev. date: 11/14/2024

DEDICATION

In loving memory of Julie Holtze, without whose gift of an interactive globe this book would not be in your hands right now.

FOREWORD

By Brad Gioia

I met Sam Waitt in the early part of 2009. His family had been living in Santa Fe, New Mexico, and wanted to make the move to Nashville to escape from what they perceived was a climate that had gone astray personally and politically in that region of the country. They longed for the more traditional values of the South and Midwest. Their roots were in Iowa, and they appreciated the values in the more conservative world of Nashville. Sam and his family had made an appointment to meet with me to discuss his transferring to Montgomery Bell Academy for his high school years, where they admired the classical approach to education.

I was struck by Sam's intelligence and curiosity. He had a mild case on the Autism Spectrum, and like most celebrated individuals with this condition Sam exhibited a poignant and striking intelligence. I was immediately charmed by his inquisitiveness, sense of humor, and innate intelligence. I knew almost immediately he would be successful at our school.

Throughout his high school years Sam invested himself in politics and history. He was always self-effacing, sensitive, and discerning, and each year his confidence and depth of interest in academic subjects took deeper root. By the time he graduated I knew he would be successful at Furman University, where he majored in political science and international relations and immersed himself in international studies. I relished hearing his conversations about historical and political topics, and I knew he would make use of these studies in a much more serious and professional manner.

What surprised me most is that Sam pursued several adventurous paths. He committed to studying Polish so he could travel to Warsaw and other cities and learn firsthand about its culture, society, and political structure. He also visited Lithuania, where he made some lasting friendships and gained personal and professional insights into the instability and fragility of Eastern Europe. During this same period Sam earned an M.A. in international studies.

Beginning in late November of 2023 Sam undertook a plan to begin a formal blog about political topics and timely world issues. His interests have ranged from the geographical advantages the United States enjoys, as well as its precarious role in policing the world and complex issues surrounding energy and oil dependence, to Russia's invasion of Ukraine and the threats to the surrounding countries, the NATO agreement and the shadow of competing superpowers such as China, Russia, and Iran, and the ongoing forces that undermine the free world on university campuses and within our Democratic ideals. It is not just Sam's astute observations that fascinate the reader but his honesty and willingness to be vulnerable, forthright, and often clever and humorous surprise us.

These twelve essays are a rich compilation of wit, wisdom, and incisive observation. At times, Sam stirs the political debate by waging Marjorie Taylor Greene against Mike Johnson or reminds of the nuances of history from America's greatness after World War II and the imagery of Norman Rockwell's painting of a Thanksgiving celebration and how much gratitude we should have in a troubled world. His sense of humor is highlighted when he introduces his essay "Georgian Nightmare" by reminding us that the word Georgia evokes images of peaches, or a famous football team named the Bulldogs, and even a famous song by Gladys Knight referring to a Midnight Train. Most of all, Sam's optimistic and kind spirit, love of history, and keen observations are all beautifully crafted in these essays.

CONTENTS

INTRODUCTION

Greetings, Readers. If you have made it this far, it means you clearly support me and my work. Thus, I hand out my deepest gratitude to you. You are about to read my perspectives not only on geopolitics, but also obtain access to my inner thoughts about how the world works today.

While I clearly have a passion for Eastern Europe and the Post-Soviet Space, as three of this compilation's newsletters focus heavily on issues in those regions, I am also aware that you may be interested in other matters, particularly if they come close to home.

As my first article indicates, I am an optimist about America's future despite all the polarization you hear about in the media. I hope you find some of my works not only enlightening but also humorous, with my specialized dry sensibilities.

Thank you again for finding the time to read my work. If you have demand for more content, I will be most happy to oblige.

FREEDOM FROM DANGER

Despite instability around the world, Americans still have much to be thankful for.

NOVEMBER 21, 2023

While we see headlines about skirmishes, tensions, and even wars on the other side of the world, we ought to be reminded of how geographically removed we are from those conflicts. America's greatest strength for more than a century has been, and always will be, our geography. Protected by the Atlantic Ocean to the east and the Pacific Ocean to the west, the United States has perhaps the greatest natural defense barrier that any nation has ever had in the history of human civilization. The protection provided by these oceans to the United States from any hostile Eurasian power has proved itself time and time again in a way that has kept our homeland safe from Eurasian conflicts. On top of all that, the United States has more than 5,000 nuclear weapons, ensuring that any hostile power cannot attack our homeland without risking its complete annihilation. Thus, so long as any of us are alive, there will likely never be a military attack on the American homeland.

Beyond the protection that two oceans and our strategic defenses provide, the United States also has another monstrous advantage – our two militarily weak and largely friendly neighbors. While many of us may have our differences with both Canada and Mexico, with the current left-wing administrations governing both nations, the overall relationship between the three nations is completely void of military hostility as all three North American countries tend to prioritize what unites us, rather than what divides us. Both Mexico and Canada, but especially Canada, are, like the United States, the products of centuries of immigration, first from Europe but now increasingly from elsewhere. This dynamic has created three societies where the many centuries-old tribal grudges still manifested on the Eurasian and African continents have softened into what I will call the great North American melting pot.

Finally, we in the United States ought to be thankful that after years of energy dependency on Venezuela and the Middle East, the United States became in 2017 a net exporter of natural gas and in 2020 a net exporter of oil. With oil and natural gas still essential to our functioning as a society, we can most certainly sleep easy knowing we will never again be vulnerable to the blackmail of a rogue dictator. Contrast our situation with that of Europe. Following Russia's 2022 invasion of Ukraine, Europe became a victim of Russian energy blackmail, and the European economy thus needed to be rescued by natural gas from the United States. While many of us have concerns about the environmental impacts of these policies, we can clearly see that unlike in many poorer countries, the skies above America are blue, the air quality is relatively healthy, and much of the breathtaking American West is still protected from development for all eternity.

In conclusion, I will take you to World War 2, when *Saturday Evening Post* illustrator Norman Rockwell painted his "four freedoms" depicting the virtues of American life as horrific conflict was raging overseas. These paintings, intended to boost the morale of the nation during challenging times, have since become iconic depictions of how lucky we really are. One of them, entitled *Freedom from Want,* depicts an American family enjoying the abundance of a Thanksgiving turkey. Fast forward 80 years, and Rockwell's painting of the blessings of America still has the same message that it did during the depths of World War 2. To conclude, this Thanksgiving season we should all truly be thankful that we live in the United States of America. There truly is no place more secure from external threats on the whole Planet Earth.

FROM RUSSIA WITH VENGEANCE

How far exactly do Russia's territorial ambitions go?

DECEMBER 13, 2023

In February 2022, Russian President Vladimir Putin executed perhaps one of the biggest blunders in all of world history. After years of attempting to halt Ukraine's drift toward the United States, European Union, and NATO with trade wars, hybrid wars, misinformation, and all other methods of blackmail imaginable, Putin crossed the line with the ultimate act of coercive power – an all-invasion to topple the Ukrainian government with military force. This heinous act surprised many Americans, Western Europeans, as well as citizens of nations many thousands of miles away from the borders of either Ukraine or Russia. However, there was a group of countries whose citizens, while shocked and horrified by the atrocities committed by Russian troops, were not surprised. For the citizens of countries such as Poland and the Baltic States of Lithuania, Latvia, and Estonia, all of whom are barely more than one generation removed from Russian dominated Soviet Communism, illogical displays of force from Russian leaders are just par for the course.

Back in 2008, the former Soviet Republic of Georgia in the Caucasus mountains was under attack from Russia. Using its proxies in two separatist regions that broke away from the new republic in 1992, Russia retaliated to the administration of Georgian President Mikheil Saakashvili's intention to join NATO by launching a full-scale invasion of the country. While diplomatic intervention by France ultimately stopped the invasion and kept Saakashvili in power, the conflict sent a chill through Russia's former satellite states. In a show of solidarity to the embattled nation, Polish President Lech Kaczynski, Ukrainian President Viktor Yushchenko, and the presidents of all three Baltic States a promptly made a visit to the Georgian Capital of Tbilisi. While there, Kaczynski uttered these words that have since become prophetic: "Today it is Georgia, tomorrow Ukraine, the day after tomorrow the Baltic States, and then perhaps the time will come for my country, Poland." Less than two years later, Kaczynski was killed in a plane crash that to this day has been suspected of being perpetrated by the Russian government.

Kaczynski's 2008 prediction, dismissed at the time as a reflection of Poland's PTSD from 50 years of occupation, proved correct with Putin's 2022 invasion of Ukraine. Even with their NATO membership and the security guarantee it offers, nations such as Poland and the Baltic States still hold deep concerns for the future. Within minutes of the initial bombardment of Ukrainian cities, Lithuanian foreign minister Gabrielius Landsbergis wrote on the website formerly known as Twitter that "We in Lithuania know it very well that Ukraine is fighting not for us in the region, Europe, and everyone in the democratic world." Also, the man currently holding the Polish presidency, Andrzej Duda, warned in an interview with *PBS* that should Ukraine collapse, Russia "will not stop. It will want to bite off other pieces of territory." Thus, these warnings from Polish and Lithuanian officials make us wonder, if President Putin really does seek more territory beyond the whole of Ukraine, how far do these ambitions go?

If one listens to Russia's warmongering TV pundits and propagandists, as well as former Russian President-turned drunken lunatic Dmitry Medvedev, the answer is quite simple – Russia has no end point for its military ambitions. Since Ukraine was attacked, such threats of invasion, missile attack, and even the use of nuclear weapons against dozens of sovereign nations have become commonplace on Russian TV. If you want to test your sanity, try watching clips of Russian State TV or reading Russian propaganda articles, as I have unfortunately done – much to the detriment of my mental well-being. On one episode on the notorious TV Program *60 Minutes* hosted by the acerbic Olga Skabeyeva, a guest pundit named Nikolai Vavilov claimed that cities such as Berlin and Paris would eventually be incorporated into a new Russian Empire encompassing all of Europe. Vladimir Solovyov, another venomous false prophet who also hosts a propaganda program went one step further – that Russian troops could go full *Call of Duty: Modern Warfare II* and take Washington, DC. Furthermore, Medvedev, through his regular social media usage of taunts and racial slurs against almost every country except for China, has also stooped to habitually threatening NATO countries with the same violent eventualities broached on Russian state TV.

How seriously should we take all these seemingly ludicrous threats? After all, in the real-world Russian troops have struggled to hold on to the Ukrainian territories they control now and seem woefully incapable of making a serious offensive deeper into Ukraine, let alone into a NATO country. I am not interested in Russian capabilities, but instead in Russian intentions. And as we can clearly see, Russian president Putin *intends* to control most, if not all of Ukraine, with the possible exception of the far western regions of Ukraine near the borders of Poland and Hungary that were never controlled by any Russian entity until after World War II. While Russia may be satisfied with these regions as a rump state with no economic viability, this does not mean that Russia's intentions stop in Ukraine. In fact, my study since February 2022 has given me every indication that several other countries remain in Putin's plans.

The most obvious that come to my mind are Georgia and Moldova – two former Soviet Republics with neither the NATO membership nor the natural resources to negotiate on an equal footing with their former colonial masters in Moscow. Of the two, Georgia may not even need to be invaded. Since Saakashvili's ouster in 2012, the small Caucasian republic has been governed from the shadows by Bidzina Ivanishvili, Georgia's wealthiest man. Since Ivanishvili made his wealth in Moscow during the chaotic years following the collapse of the Soviet Union, he sees little reason for his country to be too closely associated with Western international organizations. Thus, rather than a victim of another Russian invasion, Georgia is more likely to see more creeping Russian influence over the coming years. On the other hand, Moldova, a tiny country sandwiched between Ukraine and Romania and entirely dependent on Western aid, has been sinisterly mentioned by Russian Foreign Minister Sergey Lavrov as "the next Ukraine" used by the USA as an "anti-Russia." This sort of threat, along with allegations of a Russian-backed coup attempt in February 2023, leaves little doubt that Putin and his associates would like to swallow Moldova as well.

However, the strategic significance of Georgia and Moldova pales in comparison to three more former Soviet Republics – the Baltic States. Sandwiched between Russian ally Belarus and Russian exclave Kaliningrad, Lithuania, Latvia, and Estonia are seen as challenging for NATO to defend. Despite their small size (the three countries combined are smaller than Oklahoma), a hostile incursion into one or all the Baltic States would have dire implications for international security and the global economy, considering that they are all members of NA. and the European Union. Western countries would be faced with a no-win decision of a large-scale war with a heavily armed enemy or the collapse of the Western political and economic order as three members are yanked out of it against their will.

While neither the Baltic States nor Georgia and Moldova carry the emotional significance for neither the Russian public nor the Russian elite that Ukraine does, President Putin has one very powerful reason to want the Baltic States back. Beyond his aspiration for historical revenge against the first three Soviet Republics to declare independence in 1990, a successful Russian occupation of the Baltic states would most certainly lead to the collapse of NATO as the Article 5 collective defense clause is proven a mirage and the whole Western alliance declares geopolitical bankruptcy. I have been to Lithuania. Driving through the country you see how flat it is, how small it is (driving from one side to the other only takes three hours), and how easy it would be for the Russian army to occupy it should Western countries abrogate their obligation. That is why we must do all we can to prevent Putin or his successor from even considering such a catastrophic military intervention.

Beyond former Soviet Republics such as Ukraine, Georgia, Moldova, or the Baltic States of Lithuania, Latvia, and Estonia, it becomes quite difficult to assess how far the Russian military leadership would like to continue its imperial quest. Polish historian Daniel Botskowski claims that President Putin holds a serious grudge against not only Ukraine and the three Baltic States, but Poland as well. According to Botskowski, this grudge stems from role played by the Polish trade union *Solidarity* and the Ukrainian and Lithuanian national movements in the collapse of the Soviet Union. This historical fact, plus the stridently anti-Russian political positions Ukraine, Poland, Lithuania, Latvia, and Estonia have taken since the 1990s has only toughened the Russian president's resolve to see these countries erased from the political map as they were during the Tsarist era. While Botskowski also claims that Putin would like to control Finland, it seems unlikely to me that he holds the same kind of grudge against Finland due to Finland's long-time special relationship with Russia that only collapsed after Russia attacked Ukraine in 2022.

Rather, it has become clear to me that Putin, his militant advisors and yes-men, and Putin's likely successor view Finland, along with most countries in Europe and even outside of Europe through a similar lens. Since the Soviet Era, Russian strategic thinking has come to view the United States, Russia, and China as the only "sovereign" states, with all the others, whether they be Finland, Cuba, Germany, or Burkina Faso (where a Pro-Russian military junta recently assumed power) as pawns in Russia's confrontation with the United States. Since the Russian elite has come to believe that the United States seeks to break up Russia through popular uprisings and civil war, every country that has a military alliance with the United States is, as the weaker partner in the relationship, automatically a puppet and vassal state of the Americans. In Russia's ideal world, the larger European economies, such as the United Kingdom and Germany, whom Putin believes are under the control of the United States, should simply be junior partners to Russia as Russia dominates much of Eurasia, China dominates East Asia, and the Americans retreat back to the Western Hemisphere.

This sort of hysterical and conspiratorial thinking does not bode well for the future of international security on the Eurasian landmass. All attempts to reason with Russia to limit its militarism and reassure Russia that neither the United States nor any other country has aggressive intentions have failed. Russia's worldview — where countries of the former Soviet Union (not always excluding NATO members Lithuania, Latvia, and Estonia) are its special domain and that other countries are just pawns between the USA, Russia, and China has only hardened. Thus, to answer the question about whether Russia intends to go has a nebulous answer. Even though we might laugh at Russia's military capabilities, we must not ignore Russia's grand ambitions to shake up global security arrangements in ways where Russia calls the shots. The ambitions to control other sovereign nations, including those closer to the United States such as Cuba, remain as steadfast as they were during the first Cold War.

So, we can see that Russia would like to return all Soviet Republics, especially those who have most loudly criticized Russian policy (Ukraine, Georgia, Moldova, and the Baltic States) with the Baltics being the most dangerous flashpoint due to their memberships in NATO. For much of the rest of Europe, (with the exception of Poland due to Putin's grudge against it) and the world, Russia's ambitions are not defined by a binary "conquer or not conquer" situation, but rather viewed through the lens of confrontation with the United States, where any opposition to Russian policy is viewed in a conspiratorial manner as part of an American plot to destroy Russia. These conspiratorial beliefs, along with Ukraine's likely failure to retake more territory in the coming years, mean that we should continue to watch out for Russian ambitions, and pray that Russia is never able to attack a NATO country in the same way it attacked Ukraine. While we should not be alarmed that a Russian attack on a NATO country is imminent or inevitable, we should at least remain vigilant.

THE LAMENT OF AN ANTIQUATED CONSERVATIVE

America's credibility is under strain from both sides of the political aisle.

FEBRUARY 14, 2024

On April 4, 1949, The United States, together with Canada and ten European countries, signed the Washington Treaty as a warning shot to the Soviet Union. Since Soviet tyrant Josef Stalin made clear he sought control over not only Eastern Europe, but Western Europe as well, the only option determined by these Western countries to prevent Soviet aggression and a repeat of the horrors of the Second World War was to band together under and create the North Atlantic Treaty Organization, commonly known as NATO. The Keystone of NATO and the Washington Treaty was Article 5 – that an attack on one member automatically equates to an attack on all members. The signing of the Washington treaty, nearly 75 years ago, was one of the key moments that ushered in America's rise as not only a regional power in the Western Hemisphere, but a global one as well.

As NATO approaches its 75th anniversary in 2024, the situation has changed dramatically, and not in favor of the United States. For the first time in its history, the United States now faces an axis of Eurasian totalitarian dictatorships determined to act in a highly disruptive manner to subjugate neighboring countries, export their totalitarian models, and overthrow the United States as the global superpower. Perhaps even more concerning to me, as a believer in an American-led world order, than the behavior of China, Russia, and Iran, is America's internal decay. While on the surface the American economy seems resilient and political violence is contained to a handful of college campuses, there is a deeper rot to the system that is spread across the American political spectrum.

Over the last week, we have seen, not one, not two, but three major missteps by high-ranking US government officials that will make any informed person wonder – who exactly is in charge? During a press conference last week, President Joe Biden, long known for his gaffes and awkward behavior, claimed, to everyone's shock, that Egyptian President Abdel Fattah al-Sisi was not the President of Egypt, but in fact, the president of Mexico. The incident spawned a number of online memes, including one that both countries have large pyramids. On the same day, Biden was subject of a much more serious indictment of his cognitive abilities when special counsel Robert Hur, appointed by the Justice Department, to investigate allegations that Biden, like his predecessor, mishandled classified documents after leaving the Vice Presidency in 2017. And here we have our second misstep.

The report was humiliating. Not only did the Hur Report accuse Biden of acting in a manner that generated "serious risks to national security," but also of being "an elderly man with poor memory" too mentally incompetent to stand trial. According to Hur, "It would be difficult to convince a jury that they should convict him… of a serious felony that requires a mental state of willfulness." There simply is no spin the White House can concoct to save them from such a catastrophic exposure. Yet despite speculation that Biden could be replaced by a younger, more mentally competent Democrat for the November election, Democrats have largely stood behind their embattled leader. The third misstep is the fact that Lloyd Austin remains the current Secretary of Defense. Before his current struggles, Austin's valor during the 2003 invasion of Iraq earned him the Silver Star, and Austin continued to have a distinguished career in the US Armed Forces until his retirement from active duty in 2016. By 2024, far from being a war hero, Secretary Austin is a man fighting for his life.

Living with Prostate Cancer, a condition that Austin was diagnosed with in January, is undoubtedly a painful experience that can seriously distract from work and daily functions. There is a reason why King Charles has stepped back from public duties to care for his own health. While they share a battle with Prostate Cancer, King Charles and Lloyd Austin have one key difference. While King Charles was literally born to take his job, and waited 74 years to obtain it, Austin's job is at the mercy of the American constitutional order, and he can be replaced or resign if no longer willing or able to fulfill his duties or if his boss loses the next election. Secretary Austin has served his country admirably, but now for the sake of our national security, he must leave. Judging by the recent deadly strike on an American base in Jordan by a radical Iran-backed Iraqi militia, our enemies have received the message delivered by our medically compromised and AWOL leadership – bad behavior will no longer be punished.

Despite the deluge of negative news cycles for the Biden Administration, an even scarier news cycle appeared this week thanks to the big mouth of Biden's likely opponent – Donald Trump. For those of you who have known me for years, you know it has always been difficult for me, even with my conservative leanings and my agreement with many of Trump's domestic policies, to fully embrace Trump. The main cause of my position, despite the frustration it causes within my family, is Trump's views on international affairs. Trump has for decades, long before he announced his 2016 presidential campaign, criticized America's global alliances as mafia-style protection rackets where allies refuse to pay their "dues" to the United States, hence leaving the United States as the "sucker" subsidizing its ungrateful allies. In reality, the NATO alliance, formed in 1949 as the block to Soviet and now Russian expansionism, is not a protection racket. It is a completely voluntary association where members choose to receive the benefits of collective defense, with the United States and its massive nuclear arsenal the main pillar.

Instead, former president Trump, at a rally in South Carolina last weekend claimed that should NATO allies be "delinquent" in their NATO "fees" (no such payment system exists) he will not only refuse to honor Article 5, but actively "encourage" Russia to carry through with any hostile behavior it pleases. While the latter part was likely typical Trumpian bluster, we cannot ignore the grave implications of this bluster and what they mean for international security and stability. These ghastly comments led to widespread condemnation, with many leaders, including NATO Secretary General Jens Stoltenberg, claiming that they put lives at risk. I would also like to remind everyone reading this that the only time Article 5 was honored in NATO's history came in 2001 to support the United States after the 9/11 terrorist attacks. Any abrogation of the Washington treaty would constitute a massive betrayal of our allies, particularly those uncomfortably close to Russia who have absolutely taken their defense obligations seriously.

Before anyone comes after me, I want to be clear that Donald Trump and I agree that many countries in NATO have for years ignored investments in their defense. Instead, they piggy-backed on America's overwhelming military superiority for their national security interests. Worse, many (particularly Western) European countries spent years actively criticizing American foreign policy, effectively biting the hand that feeds them. Such ingratitude is a difficult pill to swallow for many Americans, hence why I empathize with my fellow conservatives supporting Trump's position. While criticism of European policy is deserved, it is still in the United States' core fundamental interest to prevent a major European war at all costs. Even if our allies spent zero on their defense (which I obviously would not support), preventing a Russian attack on a NATO country should be the number one priority above all else. While I apologize to anyone who has concerns with what I am writing, I must be frank that I still greatly resent that some powerful individuals do not understand such basic, fundamental principles.

So, here we are. America is at a crossroads of two unpalatable options, both of which deeply strain the international credibility of Ronald Reagan's "shining city on a hill." One path, the current Biden Administration, is a recipe for four more years of weakness, wokeness, embarrassing gaffes, and slow decline. The other path, a second Trump Administration, remains a leap into the unknown. Either way, America's credibility as the once all-powerful superpower that signed the Washington Treaty in 1949 will continue to deteriorate, either slowly or rapidly. On a final note, I want everyone reading this to know my personal stake in events in Eastern Europe. Over the past several years, I have spent time in Warsaw and Vilnius, the capitals of NATO members Poland

and Lithuania that each spent centuries under Russian domination- both the Tsarist and Soviet variants. Any leader of the (for now) most powerful nation on earth who stands down and allows Russia to use military force against them would be, in my eyes, committing the most heinous betrayal in American history. We cannot allow the sacrifices of the 418,000 Americans who perished in the Second World War to be all in vain.

LEAP OF FAITH

A deeply religious House Speaker chooses a side in the battle over Republican foreign policy.

APRIL 24, 2024

On Saturday, April 20, the United States House of Representatives finally approved, with a commanding 311-112 vote, a $95 billion assistance package to first Ukraine, but also to national security priorities in the Middle East and the Asia-Pacific, including allies Israel and Taiwan. All the *No* votes came from Republicans, a remarkable departure from the party's historical character as the stalwart of national defense. With an aggressive axis of China, Russia, and Iran threatening the United States and its allies overseas, the time for bold American leadership to maintain global security is now. For Ukraine, the aid has come just in the nick of time. Ukraine has been suffering with a nearly 10-1 artillery disadvantage, a manpower shortage, and major holes in its missile defense. After Kyiv's largest power plant was destroyed by Russian airstrikes, CIA director William Burns starkly warned that Ukraine risks complete collapse by the end of the year without American military aid.

Enter House Speaker Mike Johnson. Johnson, a devout Evangelical Christian, has been trapped between Ukraine and other allies' desperate need for military assistance and his own political survival. Due to his delay in moving forward the aid package, conspiracy theories online have claimed Johnson is just a puppet of Donald Trump, or even more outlandishly, a Russian asset. The real reason for Johnson's skittishness is something much simpler – Representative Marjorie Taylor Greene, and her threat to topple him from the speakership. Greene, already one of the most controversial members of congress, is clearly no fan of either Johnson or Ukraine. Immediately following the successful vote on the House floor, Greene trashed Johnson as a "traitor to our country" wasting tax dollars on a "foreign war." Greene has even gone so far as to repeat Russian propaganda verbatim by labeling Ukrainian officials "Nazis" who discriminate against Christians. To Greene and her *America First* followers in Congress and across the country, Johnson has committed a heinous betrayal and must pay with his head.

Following the defenestration of Johnson's predecessor Kevin McCarthy by hardline anti-Ukraine Republicans last October, then-unknown House Speaker Mike Johnson sought to solve the Ukraine problem by linking further funding for the country with strict security measures at the US southern border with Mexico. After that arrangement collapsed in February under pressure from Donald Trump, Johnson was plunged into in a catch twenty-two. With Marjorie Taylor Greene threatening to *vacate the chair,* as the speaker removal process is formally known, and reports of Ukraine's defenses growing ever bleaker by the week, Johnson's balancing act could no longer continue. Mike Johnson is a man whose Evangelical Christian faith, in the words of an anonymous Republican congressman, "guides him in every decision he makes." It was ultimately Johnson's strong faith, and the facts he received during intelligence briefings, which led the speaker to see the light.

After assuming the speakership, Johnson was invited to a meeting with four men who not only have tremendous knowledge and experience with national security, but also all happen to be named *Michael* (former Secretary of State Pompeo and congressmen McCaul, Rogers, and Turner). In this 5-Mikes meeting of divine coincidence, Johnson received a sobering lecture on Ukraine that began to turn the new speaker away from the isolationist position he held as a backbencher. Johnson also met with multiple European officials, all of whom strongly urged him to bring Ukraine aid to the house floor. The critical event that finally spurred Johnson to act, however, was his encounter with Ukrainian Evangelical Leader Pavlo Unguryan. Unguryan has, for the past several months, been traveling around the United States to meet with Evangelical leaders to expose widespread persecution of Protestants in Ukrainian regions under Russian occupation. For a man of deep faith like Johnson, such persecution of his fellow Evangelicals must be deeply unsettling.

While radicals in the Republican congressional caucus such as Marjorie Taylor Greene and Matt Gaetz continued to laugh off the intelligence, ignore European officials, and make superfluous equivalences between the Russian invasion of Ukraine and American border crisis, Johnson has consulted with both the human and divine to prevent even greater catastrophe in Eastern Europe. Those meetings, along with weeks of intense prayer, convinced Johnson that funding Ukraine was not only the moral decision, but the strategically wise decision: "I really do believe the intel, I think that Vladimir Putin would continue to march through Europe if he were allowed. I think he might go to the Baltics next… (or) have a showdown with Poland or one of our NATO allies. I would rather send bullets to Ukraine than American boys."

The argument that Vladimir Putin and his paranoid, vengeful regime would continue marching through Europe has been the strongest argument for proponents of giving military aid to Ukraine. And shockingly (or not shockingly,) people like Marjorie Taylor Greene or Matt Gaetz don't care. Rather than act like principled conservatives who have learned the lessons of history, Greene, Gaetz, and their band of merry pranksters seem most devoted to hogging media attention and reflexively opposing everything. Instead of following this destructive course, Johnson has risen to the occasion and proved himself as the adult in the room with a comprehensive picture of global security threats. With the guidance of both historical experience and his deep Christian faith, Speaker Johnson has definitively earned a place on what he would call *the right side of history.*

GEORGIAN NIGHTMARE

The country of Georgia has certainly been on my mind lately in the most troubling way.

MAY 28, 2024

When you hear the word *Georgia,* what comes to your mind? The world-famous peaches? The University of Georgia Bulldogs? Or perhaps even Gladys Knight's Midnight Train? You probably do not imagine ancient monasteries surrounded by jagged peaks, a bizarre alphabet resembling spaghetti, or brutal post-Soviet conflicts. In that case, let me introduce you to the former Soviet Republic known in English as *Georgia* and by the locals as *Sakartvelo.* Situated between Russia and Turkey on the east coast of the Black Sea, Georgia is home to 3.7 million people, a population roughly equal to the city of Los Angeles. Of the Post-Soviet Republics, Georgia has historically, along with Ukraine and the three Baltic States, pursued some of the boldest strategies in distancing itself from the newly formed Russian Federation. There is even a statue of Ronald Reagan in the capital Tbilisi whose head points to the north – a not-so-subtle slight to Georgia's former rulers in Moscow.

This distancing came to a head in 2008 when George W. Bush flirted with crossing Russia's reddest of red lines and offering Georgia a formal membership in NATO. More than 13 years before embarking on a similar adventure in Ukraine, then-Prime Minister (but in reality, still puppet master) Vladimir Putin reacted to Bush's invitation by launching a military invasion disguised as a "peace operation" which Putin claimed was conducted to protect civilians in the separatist regions of Georgia Abkhazia and South Ossetia. In reality, Putin, ever the liar, sought the violent overthrow the Georgian government of President Mikheil Saakashvili and the establishment of a government in Tbilisi more accommodating to Russian interests. Following a bloody five-day conflict that killed nearly 850 people and displaced more than 30,000, French diplomatic intervention eventually compelled the two sides to reach a ceasefire. While Saakashvili was allowed to remain in power, Russian troops have remained in Abkhazia and South Ossetia ever since – thus blocking any pathway to NATO indefinitely.

Now, more than 15 years after his war, Putin may finally be achieving his wish. Saakashvili was ousted in 2013 and quickly fled to Ukraine. In his place sits Bidzina Ivanishvili, Georgia's wealthiest man. Unlike the flamboyant Saakashvili, who now sits in prison, Ivanishvili prefers to rule the country from the shadows rather than engage in the boring formalities of day-to-day governance. In the so-called "wild 1990s" that followed the dissolution of the Soviet Union, Ivanishvili, then living in Moscow, earned a fortune in the Russian banking, real estate, and metals extraction sectors, of course with all the dirty double-dealing such business transactions would entail. As if Ivanishvili were not mysterious enough, he reaches the status of full-on James Bond villain with his collection of exotic animals, including lemurs, kangaroos, and even sharks.

While Bidzina Ivanishvili is not a Russian by birth or genetics, recent events have proven how "Russian" he is thanks to his attempt to reorient his country in the changing international system. For the last year, the former Soviet Republic has been locked in an epic political struggle. The source of this struggle has been the introduction by the ruling Georgian Dream Party to the parliament a law forcing non-governmental and non-commercial entities who receive 20% or more of their donations and revenue from abroad to register as so-called "foreign agents" with the threat of prison terms in case of failure to register. In context, Georgian Dream has few definitive principles beyond advancing Ivanishvili's personal interests. While the Foreign Agents law, if passed, would not explicitly shut down these organizations, it would allow the government to aggressively audit them, potentially creating the conditions for restricting their activities in the future. In the worst-case scenario, Georgia would be plunged back into Russia's sphere of influence. Unsurprisingly, Ivanishvili's and Georgian Dream's opponents, many of whom work closely with these groups, the proposed Foreign Agents law is no less than a Georgian nightmare.

The legislation has prompted polarizing international reactions. The US State Department is "gravely disappointed" in efforts which "could limit freedom of expression" while the European Union warned that the law, if implemented, would be "incompatible with EU values and standards." On the other hand, Moscow has expressed its satisfaction. Kremlin Spokesman Dmitry Peskov claims the efforts of the Georgian government are no more serious than the Foreign Agents Registration Act passed by the US congress in 1938 to block the nefarious activities of Nazi Germany in the United States. Speaking of the United States, the Kremlin has returned to its time-honored and highly predictable tradition of blaming outsiders, particularly Uncle Sam, for the massive protests and backlash that have rocked Tbilisi for weeks in opposition to the foreign agent's law.

There is no doubt that the Georgian people deeply oppose the Foreign Agents law, not so much for its content, but for what it will mean for Georgia's international position. A survey released last year by the *International Republican Institute* showed support in the country for membership in NATO at a resounding 79% and joining the European Union at an even more lopsided 86%, with only 9% opposed. With Brussels warning that implementation of restrictions of NGOs would derail Georgia's EU membership hopes, no wonder Georgians are alarmed. And with Ivanishvili and his minions feeling threatened by public opinion, it is also no wonder they are determined to push through the law and respond to the opposition with violence from the security forces. After all, should Georgian Dream lose the parliamentary elections upcoming this October, the corrupt Bidzina Ivanishvili risks repeating the fate of his predecessor Mikheil Saakashvili – a prison sentence. Furthermore, Ivanishvili, who has long espoused conspiracy theories, probably fears, as does Vladimir Putin, becoming the victim of a CIA-sponsored overthrow. This existential fear is why he is willing to bet the farm on an extremely unpopular law.

So, is there any hope for Georgia? After all, even without the law on Foreign Agents, Georgia's opposition remains weak and divided as the Georgian Dream employs dirty tricks such as coercing state employees to vote for them. With its domestic politics in shambles, the main solution to Georgia's nightmare must come from abroad. Judging by the bloc's helplessness against 2024's three great powers, it seems unlikely that the weak and ineffective European Union will provide Georgia's miracle remedy. I apologize to all Europeans reading this, but you know it's true. Instead, it will likely take serious diplomatic and economic intervention from the world's still (Sorry, China) most powerful country- the United States. Dual legislation proposed last week in congress offers both carrots and sticks to Tbilisi. Should the Foreign Agents bill be dropped, congress will work toward a free trade agreement with Georgia along with extra security assistance against Russian subversion. Should the bill pass, sanctions and travel bans will be unleashed against Georgian Dream officials.

For the sake of the future of Georgia, we all must support those opposed to Ivanishvili's regime, and pray he eventually faces more than just a travel ban. In my humble opinion, prison would be best.

THE KIDS ARE NOT ALRIGHT

The disturbing truth behind the recent campus unrest.

MAY 13, 2024

On April 17, 2024, hundreds of students at Columbia University in New York, an institution known for decades as a hub of radical activism, constructed an encampment on the campus demanding the school divest its portfolio from any entity tied to Israel. After failed interventions by the NYPD, the radical students refused to budge. Since then, the protests have mushroomed across the country and even the world. This major unrest has forced schools to make drastic decisions we hoped would be behind us after the COVID pandemic. The University of California in Los Angeles moved its classes online. Emory University in Atlanta relocated its commencement ceremony to more than twenty miles (32km) away from the campus. Columbia University, the epicenter of the tempest, cancelled its main commencement altogether. In the Western World of 2024, the kids are not all right.

What is happening on college campuses points to so many troubling trends in today's world that I find it challenging to know where to start. The first one of these trends is overt and aggressive antisemitism. While neither this most ancient hatred nor the straw man of false antisemitism accusations is new, the harassment against Jewish students on American campuses is perhaps unprecedented in modern America. These incidents have included threatening chants such as "go back to Poland," "We are all Hamas," "Globalize the intifada" and "From the river to the Sea Palestine will be free." For anyone with a knowledge of history, every single one of these is effectively a call for genocide. Other Jewish students have been the victims of outright physical violence. The conditions for Jewish students at Columbia have become so dire that Jewish students were "strongly" urged by a rabbi to "return home as soon as possible and remain home" indefinitely. In a supposedly modern and progressive society such as ours, such incidents are unacceptable and reprehensible.

Beyond the specter of genocide, the overall disruption is another factor which greatly concerns me. Four years ago, high school seniors were denied the right to a normal commencement. Instead, these students were forced to sit through ceremonies in masks, sometimes seated far apart, or even delayed an entire year. And now, with schools like Columbia and the University of Southern California cancelling their graduations citing "safety concerns," these students are forced to endure alternative arrangements yet again. There is no evidence to me that a majority of students anywhere, even at Columbia, are actively taking part in these highly disruptive protests and unrest. In fact, there is a mountain of evidence that a sizeable proportion of the most violent individuals are not students at all, but outside agitators. In any free and constitutional state, citizens have the right to peaceful dissent and protest. However, in my opinion, even if they do not cross the threshold of violence, overtly disrupting another citizen's daily business should not be allowed in any public venue. If we allow this, we are also allowing the most radical minority to dictate every detail of our lives.

Finally, while we see all sorts of condemnation of Israel, whose obliteration of the Gaza strip I forcefully condemn, we see nothing even close regarding Russia's continuing aggression against Ukraine. If the anti-Israel protests are the Super Bowl, the protests against Russian imperialism are third grade flag football. Meanwhile, for the future of global security, the conflict in Ukraine is far more critical. The latter conflict has been occurring for decades, or even centuries, and so long as Israel's existence does not come under an imminent threat, the United States and its allies have little interest in direct involvement in the world's oldest conflict. Meanwhile, the consequences of Russia controlling most or all of Ukraine would be dire, and not just for Ukraine and its neighbors in Eastern Europe. If one country can take over another by brute force, the world would automatically become much more dangerous; and yet these campus radicals cannot be bothered with the truth. Few can comprehend how frustrating this reality is for me.

A few weeks back, I took some heat for a previous op-ed bemoaning what I felt is a lack of awareness about foreign affairs among young Americans. Instead of being an indictment of our supposedly "hopeless" youth, I take solace that most American college students want no part in this chaos and instability. They just hope to attend class in person, achieve the best grades possible, graduate, find a satisfying career, and eventually repay their student loans. Instead, a minority of radicals are shutting down campuses, dramatically spoiling the university experience for the majority. In summary, I believe I have made clear my opinion of the unrest we have seen across college campuses in Western countries, regardless of my thoughts on the excessive nature of Israel's military operation in Gaza. Interestingly, these sorts of protests have been only marginal in Arab countries due to heavy-handed government intervention. If even Arab governments take a more rational perspective of pro-Hamas unrest than American students and outside agitators, then our universities have no choice but to engage in deep introspection about their purpose in the 21st century.

GERMANY'S HARA-KIRI

German, Canadian, and even our own leaders seem intent on our self-destruction and the victory of China and Russia.

JANUARY 22, 2024

For hundreds of years, defeated or condemned *Samurai* warriors and feudal lords would often be compelled to commit *seppuku*, more commonly known as *hara-kiri*, to avoid capture by their enemies or restore their honor from a disgrace. This excruciatingly painful process first involved thrusting a knife deep into the abdomen, followed by a grisly slice across the belly, and ultimately culminating in the Samurai's beheading by a *Kaishakunin* as an act of mercy. While thankfully the Japanese have long stopped performing this violent ritual, many outside Japan, myself included have long been fascinated with it and use the words *seppuku* and *hara-kiri* as a euphemism for any self-destructive act. Today, the policies enacted by

Western governments, both culturally and economically, I will describe as no less dramatically self-destructive than a *Samurai* committing *hara-kiri*. Perhaps the best case in point is Germany.

On Monday, January 15, as my home in Tennessee was being blanketed by nine inches of snow, more than 30,000 angry German farmers and their tractors created a blockade in the center of Berlin to protest the planned phase-out of subsidized diesel fuel. Finance Minister (equivalent of the Secretary of the Treasury) Christian Linder attempted to assuage the crowd only to be heckled off the stage. The farmers' protests have been the culmination of months of strikes across the country by rail workers, plumbers, and even Amazon delivery drivers all in opposition to the German economy's slow decline and the German government's habit of accelerating this decline. For a country that once prided itself as the #1 economic power of Europe with ambitions to rival the United States in the global economy, the fall has been swift (not Taylor) and stunning.

The main fault for Germany's decline has been its erroneous energy policy. For decades, German politicians gambled that Russia, through its Nord Stream pipeline, would be a reliable supplier of natural gas who would refrain from weaponizing its exports for political ends. At the same time, German politicians sought to rapidly transition the German economy towards complete independence from fossil fuels, with cheap natural gas from Russia being a bridge from the traditional reliance on coal and nuclear power to a utopia of wind and solar power. The German government was even so bold as to greenlight a *second* Nord Stream pipeline from Russia to Germany despite all the red flags of Russian misbehavior. Meanwhile, Russian President Vladimir Putin was quietly preparing to literally blow-up German assumptions about Russian intentions.

Enter the German Green Party (*Die Gruenen*). Following a surge in support in the 2021 national election from young voters concerned about climate change, this left-wing progressive political party agreed, with two more established political parties, to form a three-way coalition government, dubbed the most progressive in German history. After only three months in power, Russia invaded Ukraine. Suddenly, Germany's energy supply was no longer safe. Putin had actually planned to shut off the supply the very day of the invasion, only for his plans to be thwarted by two anonymous Russian officials. However, even when Putin did ultimately carry out his threat to ax German energy supplies as revenge for Germany's support for Ukraine, the Green Party was determined as ever to make the energy problem worse.

Since the 2011 Fukushima plant meltdown, Germany had committed by law to closing its entire fleet of nuclear power plants by 2023. And close them Germany did. Despite pleas from some politicians to rewrite the law and keep open the plants, Green ministers warned the other two parties that should Germany's nuclear power plants remain open past April 2023, they would promptly withdraw from the coalition and collapse the government. After all, ideology must come first over economic rationality – even if it means increased production of coal, a power source much dirtier than nuclear. The result has been that energy prices in Germany are now triple what they were five years ago, and German companies are forced to close factories. The Green Party's goal of drastically cutting carbon emissions has succeeded, but at a grim price. Germany's economic *hara-kiri* is now in full swing.

According to a German friend, energy policy is not the only self-destructive idea pushed by Green politicians. Rather than fix Germany's economic problems, Green politicians seem more focused on making the German language more "gender neutral" by adding unpronounceable "gender stars" (*gendersternchen*) to words and giving a green light for German citizens to change their gender without the approval of a judge or licensed psychologist. Also, the German Greens happen to forget that the auto manufacturing industry is the backbone of the German economy. On top of the challenges with electricity and gas prices, German car manufacturers now must cease the production of combustion engines by 2030. These policies will make any reasonable person scratch their head, owing to their complete detachment from reality. Meanwhile, Vladimir Putin and Chinese President Xi Jinping probably can't help but laughing at this German *hara-kiri*.

Of course, the Germans are not alone in these acts of lunacy. Canadian Prime Minister Justin Trudeau has been working overtime to one-up the German Greens in the field of virtue signaling. Last month, the Canadian Ministry of Employment and Social Development released new regulations mandating that menstrual products be available in not only ladies' restrooms, but *men's* restrooms as well. I must have been unaware of this biological miracle, since apparently men can now complete the menstrual process too. This sort of moral posturing that only "benefits" a microscopic slice of the Canadian population is exactly the policy that Canadians have come to expect from Trudeau. These plans include mandated racial and gender quotas, a growing alphabet of gender categories, and finally controversial carbon tax and cap-and-trade schemes that risk crippling Canada's vast oil industry, home to the world's fourth largest proven reserves. The last one will dramatically increase costs for Canadians already struggling with a housing crisis. For Trudeau, the goal seems to be not only following the German *hara-kiri*, but also making it even more painful.

Of course, while less drastic than in Germany, let alone Canada, the United States also has a concerning recent history of *hara-kiri* virtue signaling that must certainly amuse our greatest international rivals, China and Russia. In 2022, voters from the state of Pennsylvania elected to the United States Senate John Fetterman, a man only partially recovered from a stroke who frequently wears a hoodie and gym shorts *on the Senate floor*. While the Fetterman case is more of a tragedy for himself than the entire country, the state of California has stood out in its self-destructive behavior. While for now still the largest of the fifty state economies, California has done its best to drive business out of the state as it continues to accelerate its hyper-progressive virtue signaling. Perhaps most damaging of all is the ongoing *hara-kiri* of the US military. Rather than place international and domestic security at the forefront of its mission, the Pentagon is wasting more than $100 million per year on Diversity, Equity, and Inclusion (DEI) programs that have been reputed to shame white individuals for historical wrongs against minorities inflicted by individuals long deceased. No wonder that recruitment for the US military is currently at an all-time low.

In contrast to these self-inflicted *hara-kiri* policies being directed from Berlin, Ottawa, and Washington, our main rivals, China and Russia are implementing worrying strategic plans that will certainly put the West at an incredible disadvantage. While I want to make clear that I have no reservations about clean energy, I do have reservations about the unequal burden forced upon Western countries to reduce fossil fuel consumption while China, Russia, and India alone account for nearly half of the world's carbon emissions. Furthermore, rather than focus on philosophical experimentation in the military and driving recruits away, China (now the leading customer of Germany's lost Russian gas) and Russia are both doubling down on militarizing their entire societies and putting the military in control of the economy as well as implementing "patriotic" education curricula. It seems unlikely that either China or Russia will follow Western countries by legislating the minutiae of gender ideology or the sabotage of their own industrial base.

In conclusion, I absolutely believe that we in the west can still find a happy medium between the Chinese and Russian models of chauvinist nationalism and aggressive militarism and the Western models of cultural and economic *hara-kiri*. After all, the current progressive administrations in Germany, Canada, and the United States have all hemorrhaged their approval ratings and are likely to be ousted in the next elections. Still, the fact that we are so committed to committing *hara-kiri,* except without the honor, is quite troubling not only to me, but to millions of Germans, Canadians, and Americans. If we continue down this road, the only winners will be China and Russia.

MEXICAN STANDOFF

Voters south of the border plunge the nation into uncertainty.

JUNE 13, 2024

In the end, it wasn't even close. South of the border, in that nation formally known as the *Estados Unidos Mexicanos*, but commonly known as the spring break your brain blacked out, fifty-six million Mexican voters across thirty-two states stretching from the Sonoran Desert to the Mayan jungles showed up to vote in their national election. With 61% of those votes, a Jewish academic and former mayor of Mexico City with a specialty in environmental science named Claudia Sheinbaum was elected to Mexico's powerful presidency. Furthermore, members and allies of Sheinbaum's leftist MORENA party won 372 of the five hundred mandates in the Chamber of Deputies and eighty-three of the 128 mandates in the Senate. Finally, candidates from MORENA and its left-wing allies won six of the eight state governor elections, increasing their total of governorships to twenty-four out of thirty-two total. Sheinbaum is clearly a trailblazer. Beyond her status as the first female president in a *machismo* society, Sheinbaum is also Mexico's first Jewish president (more on that front later).

In a country that suffered nearly 30,000 murders in 2023 along with the assassination of a record thirty-nine political candidates in 2024, it is no surprise that violence and security was one of the top issues in the campaign. In Mexico, extortion is simply a daily fact of life. While much of the discussion about corruption and violence in Mexico revolves around the infamous drug cartels, known for their creative forms of torture, sometimes even the notoriously corrupt Mexican police take part in the racket. In summary, the security situation in Mexico is not the most encouraging to folks north of the border. With security deteriorating in the south of the border, that border has become a den of criminality, leading to more than 2.5 million illegal border crossings in 2023 and yet more crime and political division across the US. The political debate has become so toxic, congress almost did not pass vital aid to Ukraine.

The second topic of the campaign, while less discussed in the United States, is the personality of the man Claudia Sheinbaum is replacing – Andres Manuel Lopez Obrador, known popularly by his initials AMLO. AMLO, who is constitutionally limited to one six-year term, rose from humble beginnings in the oil-rich southern state of Tabasco into becoming a larger-than-life anti-establishment politician who finally won the Mexican presidency on his third attempt in 2018. Like his counterpart north of the border, AMLO publicly disputed his first defeat in 2006 on claims of electoral fraud. His supporters staged protests for months. The Trump comparisons do not stop there. AMLO, whose charismatic personality always lands him at the center of Mexico's news cycle, has a hostile relationship with the mainstream media, labeling them puppets of the conservative Mexican elite plotting to bring him down. AMLO also has little interest in foreign affairs, regularly skipping international summits and downplaying external issues in general. The cherry on top – AMLO cannot even speak English, nor has he shown much interest in learning the language of global communication.

These displays of bombast, along with his strong opposition to foreign ownership of Mexico's powerful energy sector (which he views as the theft of Mexico's wealth) have earned AMLO a scathing evaluation from the international media and foreign investors.

Furthermore, I believe that AMLO's anti-American views have led him to deliberately use migration and drug trafficking into the United States as a political weapon. Despite the negative verdict from the global elite, the Mexican *pueblo* see AMLO quite differently. According to *Morning Consult,* the President commands a 62% approval rating, far higher than Donald Trump or the world leaders more comfortable at Davos have ever received. What accounts for this popularity? After 30 years (1988-2018) of neoliberal governments who tailor-made an economic and legal framework favorable to foreign investment and maximum economic integration with the US, poverty and inequality remained endemic. A typical Mexican's life is one of misery, with long working hours for low salaries in manual labor while extortion and gang violence rip through communities. When wealthy Mexicans live privileged lives behind walls and armed guards, no wonder there is resentment.

AMLO's government has flipped the script by doubling the minimum wage and massively expanding social welfare to Mexico's poor. AMLO, never one to shy away from the cameras, has taken personal credit for impoverished Mexicans' newfound fortunes. Still, despite the change in rhetoric, AMLO has not taken the sorts of drastic measures seen in Hugo Chavez'

Venezuela that wrecked Latin America's once most-prosperous society. The main reason – Mexico's constitution. AMLO has consistently been frustrated by the constitutional limits imposed by his predecessors to institutionalize Mexico's neoliberal framework. These include protections for foreign companies, guaranteed autonomy of the Mexican Central Bank and regulatory agencies, and congressional proportional representation lest one party become too powerful. While one can debate the integrity and credibility of these agencies, neither AMLO nor Sheinbaum can hide the debacle on the Mexican Stock Exchange BMV the day after MORENA's landslide victory. This victory was so complete, that MORENA and its left-wing allies are only three Senate seats away from the constitutional majority that so frightens Mexican and international elites.

Judging by the lopsided election results, ordinary Mexicans have clearly given their approval to the country's new direction, despite the record cartel violence and foreign investor concerns. On the other hand, Mexican elites, among them Mexico's wealthy Jewish community and foreign investors are concerned for the future of Mexico as a safe place to do business. Ordinary Mexicans, suffering under widespread corruption and cartel violence, are likely to mock the elite concern that Mexico's rule of law is in danger. Mexico is thus deeply mired in polarization, giving Americans some relief that we are not alone in this worldwide phenomenon. Following the meltdown in the Mexican markets, Sheinbaum has attempted to reassure foreign investors, promising to "act with dialogue, harmony, and great responsibility." While Sheinbaum is seen as more technocratic and less charismatic than AMLO, the need to please Mexico's frustrated *pueblo* along with her former boss, Mexico's next president will have no choice but to walk the tightrope lest we have another Venezuela on our border. For the sake of American national security, we must hope President Sheinbaum chooses the path of pragmatism, not showmanship and nationalization.

MORE THAN A FLESH WOUND

Forget ruling the waves – Britain has, like Monty Python's Black Knight, become a shell of its former self.

JULY 9, 2024

If you can remember all the way back to January, I published an article previewing some of the key elections around the world in 2024. However, like any attention-seeking political pundit these days, my crystal ball proved to be quite foggy. While I correctly predicted the re-election of India's Narendra Modi and the sharp rise of right-wing, anti-establishment political parties in the European Union, this writer, like everyone else, could not anticipate the surprise elections 2024 held up its sleeve. In this three-part series, I will focus on three different national elections that have occurred all in the month of July. Those three countries are the United Kingdom, France, and Iran. This first installment is about the United Kingdom, a nation whose golden age has come and gone. I am sure many of you know there was once a time when the Royal Navy ruled the waves, and the sun never set on the British Empire. Now, Britain can barely get its own house in order.

In an act I would describe as an epic political *seppuku,* (now former) British Prime Minister Rishi Sunak, already struggling with an 18% approval rating, called an early election on July 4. No, that was not a typo. The beautiful irony of an Englishman penciling in July 4 as the day of his own political self-destruction is certainly not lost on me. And self-destruct Sunak did. With Sunak's Conservative Party, the world's oldest political party, suffering an epic, worst-ever defeat, Keir Starmer's opposition Labour Party won a landslide 411-seat majority, bucking the right-wing trend in Europe. However, far from being a triumph for progressivism, Starmer's victory is more of a symbol for Britain's decline. While many outsiders may blame Brexit, the depth of Britain's woes are significantly more far-reaching.

So how did everything go so wrong for Sunak? Here's my take — since halcyon days of the British Empire, the United Kingdom has been on a steep and likely irreversible decline. Housing has become unaffordable, with young Britons forced to live with their parents well into their thirties. The British National Health Service is in a state of collapse, with nearly ten million people on a waiting list for medical treatment or even a routine check-up, a trend no doubt accelerated by the pandemic. Petty crime and migration have also surged to record levels, pushing these services deeper into crisis every year. Meanwhile, the Conservative Party, once seen as a beacon of competence, has turned into a factory for scandals as well as prime ministers who fail to outlive a head of iceberg lettuce. Perhaps most ominously for Britain's future, the once almighty British Armed Forces have deteriorated substantially. Under Sunak's watch, Britain now has less than 150,000 active military personnel, barely one-tenth of the Russian Armed Forces. With prominent Russian figures ominously threatening Europe, even an optimist such as myself is worried.

In this cocktail of malaise, all Keir Starmer and the Labour Party had to do was promise a return to stability and competence – which is exactly what they did. However, should Starmer fail to deliver major reform, which seems likely, expect his party to become ingloriously booted out in a few years. I really hate to come across as pessimistic, but I simply see no alternative. My conclusion: the sun has sadly set on the once-great Britain.

PERSIAN DELIGHT

The Iranian people vote for a reform-minded president – will Iran's deep state allow him to implement them?

AUGUST 1, 2024

For my final edition of the summer elections series, I will discuss a recent election that came about under the most dramatic of circumstances. American officials and governments from allied governments around Eurasia have generally singled out four nations as part of an axis of rogue, destabilizing, and expansionist nations: China, Russia, North Korea, and the Islamic Republic of Iran. It is the Islamic Republic which shall be my topic of discussion today. Since 1979 when the Pro-American Shah (King) of Iran was ousted by hardline Islamic clerics with an open mission of the destruction of Israel and regional dominance of the Middle East at the expense of the United States and its allies. Especially since the ill-fated American invasion of Iraq, Iran has become more powerful than ever and has proven that it is the only Middle Eastern nation with both the will and capabilities to challenge the United States for regional domination. Domestically, the Iranian revolution has established a shadowy "deep state" of officials close to Supreme Leader Ali Khamenei and the Iranian Revolutionary Guard Corps with the muscle to ignore and overrule the will of the Iranian people. Now, I plan to give you a snapshot of this rotten regime, a dramatic turn, and perhaps a glimmer of hope for the future.

The dramatic turn came on May 19 of this year, Iranian and Azerbaijani officials celebrated the inauguration of a joint venture hydroelectric dam project on the Aras River which would provide electricity to border regions in both Iran and the oil-rich former Soviet Republic of Azerbaijan, which is located on the Caspian Sea. At this ceremony were Iranian President Ebrahim Raisi, Azerbaijani President Ilham Aliyev, as well as Iranian Foreign Minister Hossein Amir-Abollahian. Following the celebrations, the Iranian delegation departed the site in a convoy of helicopters. Shortly after the takeoff of an antiquated Bell helicopter (Iran struggles to import modern aircraft due to sanctions) from the newly-operation Giz Galasi dam, the mood aboard the helicopter quickly deteriorated from triumphant to *Oh, crap!* As the weather conditions grew foggy, the other helicopters not carrying president Raisi lost both visual and audio contact with Raisi's helicopter. Following an intensive hours-long search, the lost helicopter was found. None of the passengers or crew were alive.

Once it was clear that Raisi, the man aging Iranian Supreme Leader Ali Khamenei was reportedly grooming to be his successor, had left his earthy body, Iran was forced to organize a presidential election nearly a year before the next regularly scheduled one. Of course, Iranian "elections" are hardly true exercises of democracy. If that were true, Khamenei and the ideologues around him would have already been overthrown by the Iranian people. Anyway, of the eighty candidates who appealed to the Guardian Council of twelve hardline clerics, only six were allowed to run – 5 hardline ideologues committed to the Islamic Revolution and physician Masoud Pezeshkian. A widower of thirty years, Pezeshkian was trained as a cardiologist who became Iran's health minister in 2001 until 2005 under the moderate administration of Mohammad Khatami. Unlike the other candidates, Pezeshkian has hinted his opposition to Iran's harsh morality laws, particularly against women and has spoken of friendly relations with all nations of the world with one obvious exception. In a stunning upset, Pezeshkian defeated hardliner Saeed Jalili in the July 5th runoff, giving hope that Iran may experience positive political change.

Unfortunately, there are clearly limits to how far Masoud Pezeshkian can go in bringing about change, particularly in the geopolitical realm. Speaking of that one exception, Pezeshkian has called it the "illegitimate Zionist regime," a common terminology for Middle Eastern radicals about Israel and has expressed support for Iran's notorious *Axis of Resistance*. This *Axis*, considered by the Iranian elite as existential to the regime's survival against Israel and especially the United States, includes various hostile and threatening organizations such as Hamas, Hezbollah, and the Houthis. Indeed, it was the presence of these groups who ensured that Iranian foreign policy saw no fundamental changes even after the 2015 nuclear deal, ultimately justifying Donald Trump's termination of it. Sadly, while Pezeshkian may want to turn Iran away from the violence and destruction that Supreme Leader Khamenei, the Revolutionary Guard, and other members of the Iranian deep state have wrought on the Middle East, these hardline factions see this strategy not only as the fulfillment of the Islamic Revolution but also critical to their own personal survival.

Despite Pezeshkian's vow to dismantle the "walls built around the country" and "engage in dialogue with the world and secure (Iran's) share of the benefits of international cooperation," Iran's foreign policy will remain just as aggressive and militant as ever. Supreme Leader Ali Khamenei and the Revolutionary Guard believe that the United States, Israel, and our global allies (which they view as American and Israeli puppet states) are so fundamentally evil that Iran's interests are secured only through confrontation and regional domination, rather than Pezeshkian's vision of cooperation. Furthermore, while Pezeshkian (and in my opinion the Iranian people) are sick and tired of the militancy and fanaticism of Khamenei and the Revolutionary Guard, the regime's bloody and barbaric reaction to massive protests against it in 2022 shows how far they are willing to go to maintain their power. That is why Khamenei will certainly be able block Pezeshkian from negotiating a new nuclear deal with the United States and Iran remains locked in a perilous escalation spiral with Israel with seemingly no way out. As with the nuclear deal, Pezeshkian has little choice but to take part in the deep state's conflict with Israel.

So, what happens next? In my opinion, real change will only come in Iran after the Khamenei joins Raisi in the land of the damned. Maybe, just maybe, such a vacuum in Tehran would create an opening for a real reformer to finally pull Iran out of the cycle of war and violence it has been so committed to for decades.

HOSTAGE DIPLOMACY

Washington and Moscow hatch a deal to swap each other's prisoners – over the heads of the countries actually holding the Russian ones.

AUGUST 14, 2024

On August 1, 2024, following nearly four years of American humiliation among other developments in Kabul, Ukraine, and the Middle East, the Biden Administration pulled off perhaps the most successful diplomatic coup since it took office. For nearly six months, representatives of the American and Russian governments, implored by the families of imprisoned American citizens Paul Whelan and Evan Gershkovich, hashed out an old-school prisoner exchange that revived memories of the first cold war. The ultimate list of beneficiaries of the agreement proved to be highly comprehensive, the most discussed of which were Whelan and Gershkovich. Also released from

Russia were five German citizens and nine Russian dissidents, including three from the Navalny network formerly led by the slain Alexey Navalny. These released prisoners are now safe in Germany, where Navalny's opposition movement is headquartered. In exchange for these victims of the Russian government, Moscow, as is always the case, received a typical assortment of spooks, crooks, and spies, most notably Vadim Krasikov, a hitman hired by the Russian Federal Security Service (FSB) to assassinate a Chechen separatist in Berlin in 2019. Despite the criticism of this exchange, there is no underestimating its magnitude on multiple fronts, one obvious but the other more profound.

Paul Whelan, a Canadian-born ex-Marine living in Michigan, had spent much of the previous decade before his arrest in Moscow in 2018 for espionage as a global security director for multiple American companies. This work entailed frequent visits to Russia. Evan Gershkovich, the New Jersey-born son of Russian-Jewish immigrants, had been working as a journalist in the ever-more dangerous Moscow market since 2016, ultimately being hired by the *Wall Street Journal* in January 2022, shortly before Putin ordered his tanks across the Ukrainian border. While tirelessly working to provide honest coverage from such a hostile environment as

Russia, Gershkovich was arrested by the notorious Wagner Group in March 2023. In my opinion, Whelan's checkered past, which included a dishonorable discharge from the Marines in 2008, and the vagueness of his job descriptions signifies to me a high likelihood that Whelan was in fact engaged in some sort of espionage. On the other hand, Gershkovich, described by his friends as a committed journalist dedicated to uncovering the truth, was certainly the victim of diplomatic hostage extortion by an increasingly paranoid and militaristic Russian government. The fact that he is now safe with his family on American soil is certainly cause for celebration for all Americans.

Somewhere no longer safe for any American citizen to visit at all is, of course, Russia. In case you didn't know this already, Gershkovich's arrest on flimsy charges should be a Tsar Bomba-sized red flag against ever visiting Russia ever again. Unless your name is Steven Seagal, any American, German, British, or like-minded country's citizen who decides to enter Russia is now a potential target for arrest by the Russian security services to be employed as ransom in future dealings between the Kremlin and Western countries. As for yours truly, my highly informative and comprehensive visit to St Petersburg back in 2014, along with the extreme danger for American citizens, means I am in no rush to return to Russia anytime soon.

While in America we were celebrating the return of our citizens Paul Whelan and Evan Gershkovich to the safety of their families, the implications for our allies in Europe were more somber. While Russian prisoners were released from five NATO countries – the United States, Germany, Poland, Norway, and Slovenia, the deal was essentially negotiated bilaterally between Washington and Moscow with minimal to nonexistent German, Polish, Norwegian, or Slovenian input. Such an arrangement naturally revives the legacy of the dozens of bilateral agreements between the United States and the Soviet Union that neither superpower's allies in NATO nor the Warsaw Pact played any part in facilitating. Reports have emerged how the Biden Administration, after months of arm-twisting, effectively forced German Chancellor Olaf Scholz to agree to Krasikov's deportation to Russia, where he returned to a hero's welcome. In both Germany and especially Poland, the criticism for the prisoner swap has been harsh, with a former Polish interior minister excoriating the Polish government for deporting a Russian spy back to Russia while receiving absolutely nothing in return. Likewise, German opposition officials have admitted the obvious – the agreement will encourage the Russian government to double down on hostage diplomacy.

While both Washington and Moscow celebrated the return of their citizens, the complete humiliation of European countries has been laid bare for the whole world to see. So why were they left out? Eu rope's weakness and decline are an indisputable reality everyone agrees upon, including this author. Decades of Russian strategic thinking, shaped by the legacy of their defeat of Nazi Germany and the 20th century Cold War, has led the Russian elite to deem their nation as a strategic equal of the United States. On the other hand, European NATO countries are mere pawns and puppets of the United States – hence Russia's preference for bilateral diplomacy. Faced with these Russian accusations of vassalage, Europe doesn't even try to deny them. Rather, even the Europeans themselves admit their strategic dependence on the United States, a dependence no doubt exacerbated by the continent's irreversible decline. In more blunt terms, without Washington's security guarantee, the war-averse Europe would stand no chance against a nuclear-armed superpower with a colossal arms industry and a comprehensively militaristic culture.

In turn, Europe's dependence and decline are why Europe can no longer swaggeringly defy Washington's wishes as they did during the Iraq War. Furthermore, the United States, after years of asking both politely and aggressively pleading for Europe to take charge of its own security against a bitter and militaristic Russia, has the unfortunate obligation for the foreseeable future but to subsidize the old continent's security lest the militarily superior Russians use force against more countries beyond Ukraine. On a happier note, I must emphasize again that on balance, I see the prisoner swap between the United States and Russia as a positive development. After all, as an American citizen who has visited Russia with no real desire to return, I have no fear of being arrested and taken hostage by the Russian government. Also, I must emphasize the US government is always obliged to uphold the interests of its own citizens unjustly locked up abroad over the complaints of allies. In a world becoming ever-more confused by the day, this American will most certainly accept this silver lining.

SUMMER BOOKWORM

A slight detour from geopolitics to review some books with a historical flair I read over the summer.

AUGUST 21, 2024

The time has now come to confess an embarrassing fact about myself: I have never been much of a book reader. Even though I read journals and articles about geopolitics daily, opening a hardcover or paperback book was rarely on my priority list. If you guessed technology as the culprit for the sad existence of this hole in my life, you would be correct. While the internet allows users to constantly click around through several websites of all kinds instantaneously, an old-fashioned book, as it has been for millennia, remains fixed and stable. While I thankfully was old enough to experience a childhood before smartphones, I have still fallen victim to this unescapable and irreversible trend of the 21st century. However, in the summer of 2024, I finally found an escape. I read not one, not two, but three highly engaging stories told from a historical perspective.

Last April, I attended a political fundraiser in Nashville for a candidate for the United States Senate to represent the state of Montana. During that dinner, he discussed the history of Montana, particularly the rise of the Montana's labor movement which fought against hazardous and unsanitary conditions in the mines that long powered Montana's economy. It was in this context where I was introduced to the book *Fire and Brimstone* by Montana native Michael Punke. Along with writing *Fire and Brimstone* and serving as the US representative to the World Trade Organization in Geneva, Punke wrote a book whose namesake film you might remember: *The Revenant: A Novel of Revenge*. While I have no intention of reliving the raw 3-hour experience where Leonardo DiCaprio is attacked by a bear and crawls his way to revenge through brutal conditions, I do intend to describe what I thought of *Fire and Brimstone*.

In 1917, Butte, Montana was grimy and filthy mining town filled with a Cantina Bar of itinerant miners, including many from Eastern Europe with minimal knowledge of English. To create even more intrigue, in 1917, World War 1 was raging in Europe, leading to all sorts of ethnic tensions that local authorities struggled to contain. Worse, local newspapers did everything to sensationalize and fuel them. It was in this combustible environment where the Granite Mountain Mine caught fire, condemning 168 miners to their deaths, mostly from smoke inhalation. It was this tragedy that galvanized Montana's long-suppressed labor movement and ultimately led to the domination of mineworker unions that lasted in Montana's politics for decades. *Fire and Brimstone* was a highly engaging read I could not put down. Not only did the book have a flair for geopolitics and the macro historical trends of the time, it was also extremely well-written and perfectly entertaining. No wonder Punke's other novel attracted Hollywood's attention.

The second book I read, the only one with fictional characters, was by Nashville-based author Ruta Sepetys, entitled *I Must Betray You* about the Romanian Revolution of 1989. A complete page-turner, I read the last one hundred pages all on the same day. Not only did *I Must Betray You* give a raw, albeit fictional, account of the tumultuous final days of 1989 that saw the end of Romania's hardline socialist regime, but it also expressed in brutal detail all the hardships of living in a country where every conversation could be monitored, and shortages of basic goods were rampant.

My personal affinity for Eastern Europe only confirmed my satisfaction with choosing this book. However, you don't need an extensive background in Eastern Europe to read it, rather you just need an interest in history and social sciences.

The final book I read was Bret Baier's (with the help of a ghostwriter) *To Rescue the Republic: Ulysses S. Grant, the Fragile Union, and the Crisis of 1876.* Contrary to history's reputation of General and later President Grant as a drunk and crook who only found himself in the nation's highest office through sheer luck, Baier painted a picture of a sensitive yet daring man whose bold offensives shortened a bloody war that, had it lasted much longer, would have likely caused irreparable damage to the Union Grant dedicated his life to preserving. I also learned that Grant never even wanted the presidency but was effectively forced into the job. As for the drinking, Ulysses S. Grant was known for not holding down his liquor well, which gave him the undeserved reputation as a drunk. However, no real drunk could write down his entire life story on his literal deathbed in the way Grant did. In short, *To Rescue the Republic: Ulysses S. Grant, the Fragile Union, and the Crisis of 1876* gives a sober lesson to the reader on not succumbing to popular narratives before learning all the facts.

In conclusion, I feel most satisfied how I could finally overcome my irrational aversion to sitting down and reading books, so long as they match my passion for history and politics. Hopefully in the future I can enjoy more books as much as I enjoyed these three.

ACKNOWLEDGEMENTS

When conjuring a list of individuals to thank for assembling this compilation of essays, one question immediately hit me – whom should I thank first? After all, the list of individuals who have given me the tools to succeed is too numerous to count.

Then it hit me. I would not be in such a position had I not struck the cosmic jackpot of being born to Andrea Waitt (now Carlton) in Sioux City, Iowa. I could have been born in Iran, or Honduras, or even in the United States in a state of poverty and social uncertainty. Instead, I have been blessed with a nurturing matriarch who has not only given me eternal love and support, but also an extensive travel itinerary that ultimately imparted a deep appreciation for history inside of me.

I would also like to thank my two fathers, Norman Waitt and Rick Carlton, and my often infuriating but multitalented brother, Wesley Carlton, whose endless creativity inspires me. I would also like to thank my late grandmother, Julie Holtze, who first gave me the interactive globe I would play with for hours and hours as a child.

Thank you to my team – John Carney, Spence Maners, Crystal Stewart, and Caroline Vaccaro. Crystal and Caroline have been instrumental in the recording side of my platform, while John has been my faithful editor. As for Spence, well let's just say he is the office's best prankster – with me as a common victim.

Finally, I would like to thank all my teachers and mentors who share my profound interest in these topics, in particular David Cunningham, Brad Gioia, Tim Boyd, Jason Hansen, Marian Strobel, Danielle Vinson, and Jon DiCicco. Without this crowd, especially my family, I would have been given no chance in life, let alone publishing a book. I am eternally grateful.